# BUILDING BRAND VALUE

Trade Paperback Original First Published 2005

Designed and produced by Michael Kunhenn and Marlene Tosca

All text by Bruce Turkel unless otherwise noted

All illustrations by Bruce Turkel

ATTENTION CORPORATIONS, UNIVERSITIES and COLLEGES and PROFESSIONAL ASSOCIATIONS and ORGANIZATIONS: Quantity discounts are available on bulk purchases of this book for educational, gift or premium promotion purposes. For more information, please contact TURKEL, 2871 Oak Avenue, Coconut Grove, FL 33133-5207, 305-476-3500, bruce@turkel.info.

For information on courses and workshops; to book keynote speeches or to learn more about our brand consulting, advertising and design services, please visit *www.turkel.info*.

# Table of Contents

# Preface

I spend a lot of my time traveling around the globe speaking to audiences at business conferences. When I do, I always try to open my talk by telling my audiences exactly why I'm standing in front of them. As I see it, my job is to be generous with real information that they can use the minute they return to their offices. And if I can present that useful information in a way that is entertaining and compelling, so much the better.

My reason for writing this book was exactly the same: during the 25 years I've run an advertising agency and brand management firm, I've observed and learned quite a bit about how to build powerful messages that can compel people to buy our clients' products. And I've noticed that the same techniques that help savvy advertisers sell their products can also help people make compelling points in everyday conversations. If I can pass some of that information along in a way that is educational, entertaining and enlightening then I can help a lot of people get what they want from their careers, their relationships and their lives.

According to John Nasbitt, author of *Megatrends*:

"The life channel of the information age is communication. In simple terms, communication requires a sender, a receiver, and a communication channel."

If you've picked up this book, it's a pretty good bet that you've already got Nasbitt's first two required communication components—you have something to say and someone to say it to.

It is my sincere hope that after you've spent some time with this book you will also have the understanding and the skills you need to build your point across a clear and open communication channel.

*Bruce Turkel*

# Brain Darts Are Born

## *Introduction - How It All Got Started*

My business partner Phil and I were sitting around one day rehashing the same issue we'd talked about many times before: how could we differentiate our advertising agency from all the others?

Each time one of us came up with a point of difference, the other would name some agency that already had that same image.

• Dedication to creativity?
• Commitment to our clients?
• Emphasis on profits?

We even went to see other agencies present themselves so we could get some idea of what to do and what not to do. In Florida where we live and work, the Sunshine Law requires all business done with public money be done in the sunshine. In other words, company presentations made to win public contracts are open to the public.

Taking advantage of the unique opportunity this statute offered, my partner and I flew to Tallahassee to watch various advertising agencies try to win the state's lottery, citrus and tourism accounts.

## Great Minds Think Alike

We found that every single agency we watched, no matter how large or how small, claimed to have exactly the same four strengths:

### 1. Breakthrough Creativity

Each and every agency promised the folks in the audience that its shop would create ads designed to break through the clutter of the marketplace. But while some of the agencies did offer a fresh creative vision, most of them presented rather run-of-the-mill ideas.

### 2. Attention to Detail

Every group talked about its commitment to mastering the fine points. Three out of four even quoted the renowned international architect Le Corbusier with the words: "God is in the details."

### 3. Proactive Account Service

All of the advertising agencies we saw promised to stay ahead of the curve, proactively recommending cutting-edge programs and ideas to their clients.

### 4. Media Purchasing Power

Finally, all of the presenters assured their prospective clients that media purchasing power (their ability to buy magazine and newspaper space and radio and TV time) was stronger than the clout of any of the other agencies that were competing for the same advertising assignments.

Ironically enough, what these agencies failed to do for themselves was exactly what their clients paid them lots of money to do—differentiate their products and services from the myriad of look-alike, sound-alike choices out there.

No matter how different they actually were, each of the advertising agencies looked and sounded almost exactly the same!

So there we were, bouncing along in the 737 that was flying us home over the Gulf of Mexico after the presentations. Frustrated that we hadn't learned anything new or earth shattering, I stared out the window at the endless blue sky and blue water and mumbled something about there having to "be a good idea out there somewhere, but what is it?"

I should tell you that while I wasn't enjoying the turbulence much, my partner, who loves to fly, was almost giddy with glee. The way he looks at it, there's no other place where you get to experience turbulence so you should enjoy it as a rare treat. He also thinks that

*The way my partner looks at it, there's no other place where you get to experience turbulence, so you should enjoy it as a rare treat.*

8

"turbulence is what makes pilots earn their pay" and he liked knowing that he was getting the full value for his aviation dollar. Because I knew that my partner felt that way, I should have thought twice about asking him a serious question. But it was too late—I had already asked him what he thought we should do—and now my question was bouncing right along with us.

? My partner, doing his best Keye Luke imitation, answered sagely: "The answer is in the question, Grasshopper, and when you can grasp the pebble from my palm you can leave the temple." (By the way, Keye Luke was the actor who played Grandfather in the TV series *Kung Fu*.)

"The answer is in the question. The answer is in the question." What in the world does that mean?

Because I had no better suggestions to work with, I took Phil's sarcastic advice to heart. Back in our office I decided to see if the answer was indeed in the question after all. So I went through our archives, gathered up a good sampling of fifteen years of our work, and spread it out on our big black Italian conference table. Peering over a steaming cup of coffee at all those years of hard work I tried to figure out exactly what made our work special.

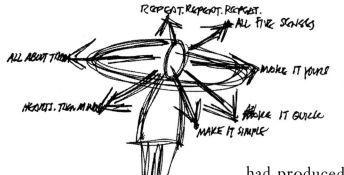

And—KABOOM!!—lightning struck.

What I found, standing there with years and years of our work laid out around us, was that the most successful campaigns we had produced, the ones that had garnered the most attention and sold the most products, were the ones with the simplest, most direct messages. And of all those great campaigns, the ones that did the best job selling our clients' products and had achieved stellar results, were the ones that were instantly recognizable and memorable.

It was a revelation.

As I looked at the work and thought about what was becoming so obvious, I noticed another common trait in the group of very successful ads spread on the table. Those ads didn't focus on the product they were selling — instead they were clearly aimed at the person they were selling to.

Excited and energized, I spent the next few weeks searching through archives of advertising and industry publications, cataloging the traits that I thought made for the strongest communications.

The theory held!

*The campaigns that did the best job selling our clients' products were the ones that were instantly recognizable and memorable.*

*In a flash of pure inspiration,*
*we labeled our best advertising messages:*

# The Seven Points of Brain Darts

L et's get right to it, shall we? What I found in those first heady days, and what we've expanded, developed and confirmed through more years of creating and learning is that the steps to creating a great brand can be characterized by seven key points:

1. All About Them.

2. Hearts Then Minds.

3. Make It Simple.

4. Make It Quick.

5. Make It Yours.

6. All Five Senses.

7. Repeat, Repeat, Repeat...

You'll notice that each of these points can be expressed in only three words. Explaining what each one means takes a few more words, but it's all quite simple.

# 1. All About Them.

People care most about things that affect them. In order to reach them you need to communicate in a way that answers their question "what's in it for me?"

# 2. Hearts Then Minds.

People make decisions based on their emotions and justify their decisions with the facts. If you want to get someone to pay attention to the intellectual reasons why they should do something, you must get them emotionally involved.

# 3. Make It Simple.

Today's world is a busy, confusing place. If you want to make an impression and an impact, your message must be succinct and digestible. Most importantly, it must immediately present the core essence of your point.

# 4. Make It Quick.

The taciturn comedian Stephen Wright said that if you put instant coffee in a microwave you'll go back in time. That may be an exaggeration, but the truth is that things happen so fast these days that if you take your sweet time, no one will wait around for you to present and explain your entire hypothesis.

## 5. Make It Yours.

A message is truly powerful only if it is associated with you or your product. Make sure that the message you're presenting belongs only to you.

## 6. All Five Senses.

Conversations involve all of the human senses. To communicate effectively, you must be sure that you're engaging as many of your audiences' senses as possible and that you're doing it in a positive way.

## 7. Repeat. Repeat. Repeat...

For a message to be effective, it must be stated, supported, and enforced. Be sure that your message is repeated often enough that your audience can consider it, digest it, internalize it, and act on it. Ironically, this doesn't give you license to be boringly repetitive. Instead, you must look for new and creative ways to repeat and reinforce your position.

Granted, not every communication that embraces these seven principles can be called a Brain Dart, and not every single Brain Dart uses all seven of these points. But when these seven points are used to create clear, direct communications, the resulting effort will produce superior results time and time again.

Most importantly, the practice of creating Brain Darts isn't just for advertising. It succeeds fabulously in all interactions where it is important to secure attention, get a point across, and entice the listener towards your point of view. Conversations, speeches, presentations, essays, and explanations can all benefit from our seven Brain Dart principles.

It's important to note that while these seven points are presented in a casual, friendly and simple manner, that is by very careful design and should not be taken to suggest that the program itself is casual. I doubt that the words Moses brought down from Mount Sinai on carved tablets would have had the same ability to change the world if they had been called the Ten Suggestions instead of the Ten Commandments. Likewise, our Brain Dart principles should not be used only when convenient and discarded when things become difficult. They should become the cornerstone of your communication planning, creation and implementation.

## *Going Topless:*
## *An example of a perfect Brain Dart*

Sometimes Brain Darts can hit close to home.

When the lease expired on my last car, I told my wife that I wanted to get another convertible. This probably came as no surprise to her since I'd already had six convertibles and she knows how much I enjoy driving with the top down. Still, her first response was that maybe I should reconsider my choice because "the kids are getting bigger and convertibles aren't so safe."

While her concern for our kid's safety made good sense, her comments didn't. Why was safety so important now that "the kids were getting bigger?" Was it because when they were small they hadn't been with us for long we weren't as attached to them? Or was my wife concerned that now that "the kids were getting bigger" their heads would stick up dangerously above the windshield? Truth is, safety seemed like an odd concern because I have a good driving record and have never wrecked or flipped any of my other convertibles. Still, on an emotional level, I could certainly see why she was troubled about me driving with our kids in a car that substituted a canvas tarp for a steel roof.

And then, driving home from the airport with my wife one evening after returning from a speaking engagement, I saw a billboard for a beautiful new convertible. The car was posed with its top down, sitting on the beach surrounded by umbrellas over the brilliant headline: "Tan Safely." I pointed to the beautiful blue car on the billboard and asked my wife what she thought of it.

"Oh, a Volvo?" she said. "A Volvo convertible? I didn't know they made those. A Volvo convertible. That's great, Volvos are safe."

Of course! A Volvo convertible was exactly what I needed.

It combined the open-air motoring I wanted with the reassurance of safety that my wife wanted me to have. A perfect compromise.

It was also a perfect Brain Dart, because for years and years Volvo has hammered home the message that their cars are safer. Volvo's marketing team understands the power of Brain Darts.

## 1. All About Them.

Volvo knows to make the pitches for their cars all about what I care most about—keeping my family safe, happy, and healthy.

## 2. Hearts Then Minds.

Sure, there are many technological reasons why Volvo deserves its reputation for safety. But before they could sell me on those facts, they needed to tug at my heartstrings, which they did by implying how safe my children would be in one of their cars.

## 3. Make It Simple.

The difference between confusing your listener and making your point is often the difference between filling your communications with extraneous information and getting right to the point. Volvo *Makes It Simple* when they promote one thing: SAFETY.

## 4. Make It Quick.

Volvo really understands this. Their Brain Dart, Safety, is only one word. And their tagline, For Life, is only two. What could be quicker than a word or two?

## 5. Make It Yours.

There's no question that Volvo owns the safety positioning among car manufacturers. Want proof? Ask anyone to tell you one word that describes a Volvo. They'll all say the same thing: "Safety."

## 6. All Five Senses

Synesthesia is when a sense impression is created by an appeal to another sense. Advertising for convertibles utilizes this by describing the wind in your hair, the spray of the surf, or the scent of freshly mowed grass. I experienced synesthesia when I saw that Volvo billboard, felt the sun on my arms and smelled the open-air world all around me.

## 7. Repeat, Repeat, Repeat...

Volvo certainly understands this last point of Brain Dart. They've been talking about one thing—safety—for as long as I can remember.

## If You Talk The Talk,
## You'd Better Walk The Walk

Unfortunately for Volvo, in 1991 they violated the sacred trust they held with the public with their safety positioning, and they paid dearly for their mistake.

Remember the ad in which a giant customized pickup truck drove over a row of automobiles? The monster truck crushed all of the cars except a Volvo station wagon that was unscathed. When The Federal Trade Commission found "the Volvo was structurally reinforced and that the structural supports in the other cars were severed"[1] and that the advertising was misleading, Volvo had an enormous PR nightmare on its hands.

All of a sudden, BMW, Mercedes, Saab and others (Cadillac promised "Not Just An Air Bag, An Air Curtain.") started treading on Volvo's territory by selling advanced safety devices. They were handed this opportunity because Volvo had violated its sacred pact with consumers— Volvo's safety positioning had been compromised.

Volvo could no longer sell ugly cars by touting safety. Remember what Dudley Moore's character said about Volvo in the movie *Crazy People*? "Volvo. They're boxy, but they're safe." Because Volvo violated its core value— safety—the company had to start designing beautiful cars. To make their line more appealing, they even came out with the turbocharged convertible I bought.

[1]Volvo North America Corp., 5 CCH Trade Reg. Rptr. Par. 23k,041 (1992)

# Point #1 *All About Them*

## *Making Beautiful Music Together*

My ten-year-old, Danny, had a problem at school. No matter what he tried, he just couldn't get along with his music teacher. Every day he came home complaining that she yelled at all of the students in the class, that she expected them to learn difficult passages on their plastic recorders, and that she constantly questioned Danny's interest and ability.

Ironically, this was the same child who had been taking classical guitar lessons since he was seven years old and had been told by the director of the Music Department at the University of Miami (where he was the youngest member of the youth guitar orchestra) that he had perfect pitch.

Because he was having such a difficult time in music class, he was ready to give up on music. Danny didn't want to practice his recorder or even his guitar anymore. He was frustrated with his music teacher and couldn't see any way out of his dilemma except to have my wife or me sign a waiver excusing him from music class.

Instead I suggested a different strategy: "Why don't you try to build up a good relationship with your teacher?" I asked. "If she knew how much you loved music and how much time you spend listening and learning, maybe she'll change her ways."

"No way. It won't work," Danny complained. "She's mean and she hates me. There's nothing I can do. I just want to get out of the class. I hate music."

"Look, Danny," I counseled, "it doesn't make sense that a kid who loves music as much as you do shouldn't enjoy his music class. And it doesn't make sense that a teacher who loves music as much as she must wouldn't be thrilled to have a kid like you in her class. It seems kind of silly that you and your teacher don't get along, doesn't it? Maybe we just haven't tried the right approach. Let's try an experiment—and see if together we can change her outlook. It'll probably…"

"No way!" Danny interrupted, "It won't work. She hates me and she'll yell at me if I even try to talk to her."

"Okay, maybe she will," I conceded, "but you've told me she hates you already and that she's mean. She'll probably yell at you whether you try something or not, right? So if you try to talk to her and she yells at you, you're not any worse off, are you?"

Danny shrugged. "I guess not," he said reluctantly.

"So?" I asked.

"So I've got nothing to lose, right?" my son said.

"You're right, but maybe, just maybe, if you try something new she'll respond to you in a new way too. And maybe, just maybe, you'll be pleasantly surprised."

So let's try this: you know that new tune you were writing, the one that used the chords from that Limp Bizkit song you like so much?"

Danny nodded again, more interested now that I'd mentioned his favorite band.

"Play it for her and ask her about that chord progression you're having a problem with. Show her that you're interested in music and interested enough to write your own songs. More importantly, show her that you appreciate her talents, that you look up to her, and that you're turning to her for help because you respect her."

"But I don't," he shot back.

"Yes you do. You have to respect someone who knows as much about music as she does. You just don't like the way she treats you. But I don't think you question her knowledge, do you?"

Danny shrugged.

"So let's try to change the way she treats you. Remember, you already told me you have nothing to lose."

When I finally agreed to go with him to talk with his teacher, Danny promised to try a new approach although he made it very clear he was convinced it would not work.

Of course you can guess the rest of the story. Danny and I went to his school, met with his teacher, and he showed her the composition he needed help with.

She not only helped him figure out the chords and harmonies he was struggling with, but the two of them got so wrapped up in the project that neither one saw me leave the classroom.

Danny's teacher was so taken with his initiative (and his interest in her abilities) that she organized a special elementary school band that met each Wednesday at seven o'clock in the morning, on her own time! By the end of fourth grade, the group was accomplished enough that she had them play Rockin' Robin at the annual student music festival—with Danny wailing away on lead guitar. And it all happened because his teacher was approached in a new manner that built up her own self-image and made the effort to change her behavior worthwhile to her.

Truth is, people are most interested in how things affect *them*. Even though none of us like to think of ourselves as selfish or egocentric, most people still tend to see things in terms of their own self-interests.

*People who care about what we have to say make us feel good about ourselves… these are the people who receive our attention, our affections, and our business.*

Because we go through life trying to maximize our pleasure and minimize our pain, we respond favorably to others who seem interested in helping us reach our goals. People who care about what we have to say and who value our experience and our viewpoints make us feel good about ourselves. And these are the people who receive our attention, our affections, and our business.

## Filter Me This:

People go through life wearing filters on their eyes, their ears, their mouths, and their minds. These filters alter everything they say, everything they hear, and everything they think.

More significantly, a speaker's filtered words are then interpreted by a listener who is hearing and thinking with his own filters. It's a wonder we can communicate at all!

Danny's filters, shaped by his teacher's constant haranguing, made everything his teacher said sound like a criticism. And her filters, most likely conditioned by her feelings that she had squandered her education and talent on uninterested elementary school kids, made everything the children said sound foolish, annoying, and like an enormous waste of her time.

### What materials are our filters made of?

They're constructed from layer upon layer of our unique experiences, our insecurities, and the other psychological flotsam and jetsam that make up our histories and our personalities.

If we are optimistic by nature, we tend to hear things in the best light.

If we are pessimistic, we tend to take most news with the most negative of viewpoints.

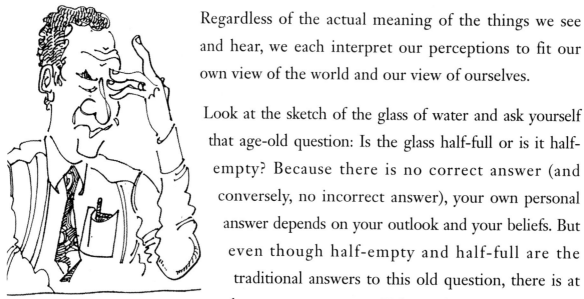

Regardless of the actual meaning of the things we see and hear, we each interpret our perceptions to fit our own view of the world and our view of ourselves.

Look at the sketch of the glass of water and ask yourself that age-old question: Is the glass half-full or is it half-empty? Because there is no correct answer (and conversely, no incorrect answer), your own personal answer depends on your outlook and your beliefs. But even though half-empty and half-full are the traditional answers to this old question, there is at least one more answer. When I showed this sketch to Danny (who was eight years old at the time) and asked him if the glass was half-full or half-empty, he glanced at the drawing and instantly answered: "It's both!" (I should add that he accompanied his answer with a look that suggested that I was daft for even asking). Danny's life experiences and his view of the world led him to the refreshingly realistic conclusion that anything was possible and that almost any circumstance had the potential to turn out to be either good or bad.

Think back to the last argument you had with someone. Better yet, think back to the last time that you tried in vain to explain something that seemed so obvious to you. No matter what facts or arguments you used, the person you were talking to just couldn't seem to see it from your point of view. And the most frustrating part was that not only were you right, but that it was all so simple—if only they could see it.

Unfortunately, you were explaining something that had meaning to you without realizing that the person you were talking to didn't hear what you were saying the same way you did. You were applying your unique filters to your words—and the other person was running your words through their special filters. The end result was that you were having two different conversations at exactly the same time.

How much easier and clearer it would be if we all spoke the same language and heard things the same way. But because that's unlikely to happen anytime soon, the key to creating meaningful communications is to make sure that our messages are always *All About Them*.

From now on shape your conversations, explanations, and even your arguments from the point of view of your listeners. Instead of telling them what you care about, tell them what they care about. Make sure that your points are built not from your interests, but from theirs.

Know your intention. Is your goal to win an argument, get someone's attention, or sell something? Structure your *All About Them* conversation to meet your needs by meeting your audience's needs.

In order to make your argument *All About Them*, phrase your words in such a way that the listeners can immediately see how their own personal self-interests will be served by listening to you and by seeing things your way (which they should see as their way if you phrase your words properly).

*Is the glass half-full or is it half-empty? Your own personal answer depends on your outlook and your beliefs.*

## *You Could Be A Winner!*

An easy way to make your remarks *All About Them* is to start your comments by highlighting the benefits that you're offering the listener. Similar to the sweepstakes envelope that screams: "YOU COULD BE A WINNER," a message that instantly telegraphs its advantage for the reader attracts attention. Like fish circling attractive bait or moths buzzing a shining light, listeners and readers find it easy to pay attention to messages that promise them benefits.

*An easy way to make your remarks* All About Them *is to start your comments by highlighting the benefits that you're offering the listener.*

In a conversation, this can be as easy as starting your talk by telling the people you're talking to how they will benefit from seeing things your way. Begin with an opener such as this: "I think you'll be real happy with what you're going to hear…" or "Because you care about this, you'll really get a kick out of the following suggestion…"

In a presentation, you might make it *All About Them* simply by listing the things your audience will learn from you. Start by telling them how those things will make their lives better. "My goal today is to give you some useful information that you can put to work just as soon as you return to your office on Monday."

In advertising, making your message *All About Them* might be as easy as showing the reader the result a consumer buying your product will enjoy, rather than telling them why your product is better than the competition's.

Business people often talk about ROI—Return On Investment—as the right criteria to use when evaluating a business proposition. I'd suggest that evaluating a proposition's MOI—the French word for ME, as in "What's in it for ME?"—is a better way to predict success.

**ROI**
**MOI**

### *Diapers Protect Babies.*

Speaking of advertising, diaper ads are an excellent example of Point #1 *All About Them.*

For years diapers have been sold with the obvious message that diapers protect babies. In order to protect babies, diapers are manufactured to be extra absorbent, are made from hypo-allergenic materials, or are slathered in lanolin because, as my daughter Aliana said when she was five years old: "Babies poop and peep."

The strategy is simple enough that it bears repeating: Diapers protect babies. Diapers protect babies. Diapers protect babies.

It all makes perfect sense until you realize that babies don't want to be protected. Babies like to poop and peep. It's what they do. Actually, babies do about five things: they eat, they sleep, they cry—and they poop and peep.

Yeah, I know what you're thinking. If babies like to poop and peep so much, then why do they cry afterwards? It sure doesn't sound like they're enjoying themselves, does it?

Well think about it for a minute. Babies can't talk, so instead they communicate by crying. After they've pooped and peeped they want the world—or at least Mom and Dad—to know about it. So they cry.

One day, some smart advertising executive realized all this. She figured out the way diapers were sold was all wrong. Diapers didn't need to protect babies because babies would be perfectly happy leaving their little messes wherever they make them. If all that parents were interested in was protecting the baby, then they'd line their houses with soft tiles, install a big drain in the middle of the floor, and let their babies relieve themselves whenever and wherever they felt like it.

You see, diapers don't protect babies. Diapers protect cribs, sofas, carpets, playpens and car interiors, not to mention Mom's, Dad's and everyone else's clothing.

Parents want to contain their babies' mess. Parents of infants don't want their adorable little darlings ruining their brand new white couches and plush carpets with stains and odors. And so the ads that had once listed all of the baby-protecting features of diapers—lanolin to soothe irritations, smooth edges to protect soft skin—all of a sudden focused on the diapers' absorbent layers and their ability to hold in the babies' mess.

The new strategy featured diapers constructed with special elastic cuffs, customized moisture reservoirs, and other innovations designed to keep the baby's offending materials inside of the swaddling. In other words, consumers bought diapers because they could keep the mess in the diaper and off of Grandma's new couch or the interior of Dad's Corvette—or his Volvo convertible for that matter.

Building on the success of this strategy, another smart ad person realized that diapers protected something else—something more intangible but no less important.

Remember what babies do after they soil their diapers? They scrunch up their little faces and cry. And because babies don't know the difference between night and day, they cry when their parents are asleep. After all, when the baby wets himself and wakes up, it's dark and he's alone. Babies don't like this. They want to be with the folks they like best—their Mom and Dad. So babies who soil their diapers in the middle of the night scream bloody murder because they're cold, wet, and lonely and because they want to get their parents' attention.

Mom and Dad, though, aren't thrilled to be awakened. And so they play eyeball hockey, each parent peering out of half-closed eyes while they silently pretend to be asleep and hope their partner will take care of the baby.

When one of the parents can't stand the crying anymore, they angrily tumble out of bed and trudge off into the baby's room to change the dirty diaper. And when they do climb out of their warm bed and stomp down the hall, whom are they most upset at?

The baby? Of course not.

The person they're upset at is the spouse still comfortably tucked into the warm bed and snoring blissfully beneath the covers.

So diapers that keep babies dry and keep the baby from waking up can protect something besides the room the baby is in. By letting the baby sleep, diapers protect a parent's ability to sleep. Think about the awakened parent grumbling at their sleeping spouse as they trudge down the hall. All of a sudden, diapers protect marriages!

Once this strategy was uncovered, diaper ads started talking not just about the diaper's ability to keep the room dry, but also about how diapers could keep baby dry and asleep.

Complicated charts and graphs showed how the latest diapers used layers of carbon fiber and activated charcoal to "whisk wetness away" from baby's bottom. And all of this incredible "anti-wetness technology" was designed not just to protect the baby's skin but also to protect the baby's sleep! And so after baby was shown sleeping quietly on clean and dry white sheets, Mom and Dad were shown sleeping blissfully as well.

Everyone was happy. Especially the diaper manufacturers, who now had a whole new reason for consumers to buy their products.

Making the diaper ads *All About Them*, all about the concerns of the people buying the diapers, made the ads work. And this very same strategy will work to get past your audience's filters and make sure that the directive you think you're projecting is the same message they're hearing. Create messages designed to tell listeners what's in it for them—why they should listen to you and respond to what you're saying. This way you'll flush out the filters and open the channels to clear and effective communication.

## *What You Can Learn From Your Bathroom*

Think about your medicine cabinet.

Open the doors and you'll find shelves stocked with bottles and boxes, potions and lotions, balms and salves. And except for the occasional houseguest who might peek into your secret stash while the flushing toilet disguises the sound of their indiscretion, nobody sees the contents of your personal medicine cabinet but you.

Still, when you close the doors and look at the cabinet, what do you see reflected in the mirror?

Nothing complex.

Nothing messy.

Nothing, in fact, but your own reflection staring back at you.

It's an interesting image because, after all, that's what the medicine cabinet and its contents are for—you.

Everything in the cabinet is there to help you tame unruly hairs, eliminate unwanted smells, and conquer unwelcome eruptions. In short, the contents of your medicine cabinet help you face the day and the night.

The best communication should be like that cabinet.

*Even though your messages are created with lots of different ingredients, their entire focus should be all about the person they are created for.*

One of the best ways to accomplish this is to know your audience as well as possible so that you can make sure you're talking directly to their needs and wants and you're appealing to their most fervent hopes and dreams.

### It's Not What You Know...

A fond childhood memory: each time we finished dinner at a Chinese restaurant, my dad would crack open his fortune cookie, adjust his glasses low on his nose, and read his fortune. "Help," he'd exclaim with mock horror, "I'm being held hostage in a fortune cookie factory."

So it should come as no surprise that years later, when we had a family dinner at our favorite Chinese restaurant and my dad pushed his chair away from the table and started to read his fortune, we all chimed in. "Yeah, yeah, we know, we know. You're being held hostage..." Instead of responding to our heckle, my dad finished reading his fortune and slid it across the table to me.

I've kept it in my wallet ever since:

A wise man knows everything.
A shrewd man, everybody.

Sure it's easier to craft messages when you know as much as possible about a subject, but when your goal is to make your message *All About Them*, what's more important is to know as much as possible about the person you're talking to.

What do they care about? If you don't know, find out.

What keeps them up at night? What gets them angry? What scares them? What excites and inspires them? What makes them laugh and cry?

How do they see themselves and what do they value?

What pain do they desperately want healed?

Knowing the answers to these questions—and communicating that understanding—will help you create messages that people will pay attention to.

# Point #2 *Hearts Then Minds*

## *"Just The Facts, Ma'am"*

From the time we first enter kindergarten as impressionable five-year-olds, we're raised to believe that facts and details are the most important things to learn. We're taught to memorize lists of spelling words, flash cards with multiplication tables, and the capitals of states and countries. And to measure how well we're doing in school, we're repeatedly tested to see just how much information we've retained.

So it should come as no surprise that when we communicate with others, we're quick to pepper our speech with facts and figures, and when we try to convince people of our point of view, we often bombard them with information that supports our argument.

When we fill our speech with volumes of information, we're mainly confusing or boring our audience. While most non-savvy marketers think it is the other way around, most people make decisions based on their feelings and then they justify those decisions with the facts.

*Most people make decisions based on their feelings and then they justify those decisions with the facts.*

Let's say you're standing in the checkout line at the grocery store. You've stacked your food on the conveyor belt and you've already flipped through *The Enquirer* and *The Star*. Setting the magazines back, what product do you notice the grocery store conveniently stacked on the aisle on either side of you? Of course! Piles and piles of impulse items, mostly candies and sweets. As you reach for the Snickers bar that's calling your name, the facts tell you the candy is loaded with calories and fat. But it sure will taste good, won't it? And it's so easy to give in to temptation and toss the candy bar onto the checkout counter with all the other things you're buying.

Point #2 *Hearts Then Minds*, will show you how to tailor your communications to make sure that you capture your listener's interest with a powerful emotional appeal before you try to capture their intellect with information.

## The World's Most Beautiful Woman

You would think that one of the most important matters consumers consider when making a purchase is price. After all, we all like to save money and we're all wary of being ripped off. And so you'd think that we'd be more likely to choose the least expensive of similar products if we had the choice. But there are at least three industries where the likelihood to purchase is directly related to the product being more expensive than its competitors. In those cases, cost actually adds value to the product: corporate consulting is one; diamond jewelry is another; perfume is a third.

Just as a CEO of a large Fortune 500 company would be unlikely to hire a consulting firm that only charged seven dollars and fifty cents an hour for its professional advice, few men are willing to ask the woman of their dreams to marry them with an inexpensive diamond. Because most of us have no idea what a diamond should cost, and because we certainly can't put a value on the love that the stone represents, the diamond industry has stepped in to tell us how much we should pay.

Who decided that the right price to pay for a rock is two month's salary? What if your salary is much bigger than mine? Does that mean that your love deserves a bigger diamond than mine? And if I got lucky and found a flawless 2-carat diamond at a garage sale for nine dollars, would it be wrong to present it to my fiancée?

How may men would dare bring home a Valentine's Day gift of perfume for their wives and announce: "You'll love it, honey. It smells really swell. And here's the best part—the entire 55 gallon drum only set me back 12 bucks!"

Without even knowing it, the fragrance industry was one of the first to embrace the entire Brain Darts concept and use it to sell their wares. That's because they inherently understood the concept of selling their products by appealing to their audience's feelings instead of by appealing to their customers' intellect. After all, few product decisions are more emotionally based than $160 billion-a-year international cosmetics and fragrance sales.

According to *The Economist* magazine: "Americans spend more each year on beauty than they do on education. Such spending is not mere vanity. Being pretty—or just not ugly—confers enormous genetic and social advantages. Attractive people (both men and women) are judged to be more intelligent and better in bed; they earn more, and they are more likely to marry..."[2]

L'Oréal knew what it was talking about when it said, "Because I'm worth it."

Think back to almost any perfume advertising you can remember. Now that you're aware of Point #1 *All About Them*, you've probably already realized that the fragrance manufacturers don't usually mention what's in the bottles of the scents they sell. Instead they go on and on about what their fragrance can do for you:

Wear Charlie or Tommy and you'll feel young.

Splash on Jovan Musk or Versace and all of a sudden you're daring and sexy.

A dash of Byblos or Gucci will make you feel sophisticated.

Douse yourself in Cartier or Chanel No. 5 and you must be very elegant indeed.

With all the photos of beautiful people frolicking together in Cannes, South Beach, and New York, not one of the perfumeries ever mentions the ingredients in their bottles.

And with good reason.

[2] *The Economist*, Pots of Promise May 22nd 2003

Besides the fact that we care more about what a bottle of perfume will do for us than what's in it, the plain truth is that what is in many perfume bottles is not all that sophisticated, elegant, or even palatable.

Do you know what's actually in a bottle of perfume?

Along with the source of the various fragrances in perfume—rose petals, let's say, or citrus peel, perhaps—and besides the coloring and alcohol that fill most of the bottle, there's something else that makes perfume, perfume.

When prehistoric cavemen roamed the earth, long before civilization began to tame its wild ways, Homo sapiens behaved as much like animals as humans. As such, they relied on their most primitive sense, their sense of smell, much more than we do today. Like the wild animals they lived among, ancient man used his sense of smell to help find food, detect fear, and identify potential mates. To do this, he sniffed for pheromones.

*"... substances secreted by many animal species that alter the behavior of individuals of the same species. Sex attractant pheromones, secreted by a male or female to attract the opposite sex, are widespread among insects. The pheromones produced by males include a substance produced by cockroaches that attracts females and orients them in the correct mating positions. Male-attracting pheromones have been discovered in the females of many species of beetles, bees, and moths."* [3]

40

[1]Pheromones. The Columbia Encyclopedia, 6th Edition. 2001

Pheromones are the chemical compounds that animals excrete to attract potential mates and to ward off other animals that might be a threat. When a male cat marks its territory, it sprays pheromones to alert other animals to its territorial superiority. When two dogs warily approach each other and circle around sniffing each other's rear ends, they are smelling and evaluating each other's pheromones.

## *Like it or not, as civilized as we think we may be, we're no different than the animals we evolved from.*

While it may be inappropriate to circle a new acquaintance, squatting and sniffing to catch a whiff of their pheromones, we still have little control over the influence of our primitive sense of smell. That explains why a quick whiff of mom's cooking, or the acrid smell of burning leaves, or maybe the warm smell of art school paste can dredge up a stirringly realistic childhood memory.

Perfume manufacturers know about the hidden power of our sense of smell and our subconscious reactions to pheromones. In fact, they study the ways they can expand upon and exploit this instinct. And so they add pheromones, either from an animal or from a test tube, to their perfume formulas.

It's not so difficult to figure out where synthetic phero-mones come from—they are created in laboratories and are intended to mimic the effects of the real thing. Gathering real pheromones, though, is a little less appetizing. Suffice to say that the compounds are often extracted from the back end of a muskrat and that the process sometimes requires a harness and a cattle prod-like device.

Now I must admit I've never seen a muskrat up close, but judging from the fact that the muskrat has the word "rat" in its name, I can't imagine that they're very attractive—to me, the word rat suggests a horrid little rodent with beady little eyes, sharp scrabbly claws, and a long scaly tail. Based on that description, I'd venture that the whole practice of extracting musk oil is not one I'd want to watch. But regardless of the procedure, the muskrat's pheromonal extracts are vital to the production of quality perfume.

If musk oil is so important, then wouldn't it make logical sense for the perfumeries to advertise that fact? After all, a comparison of the amount of muskrat-extract in a bottle of perfume might be an effective way to demonstrate a fragrance's superiority.

Imagine the commercial:

Announcer (with an elegant English accent):

*"And now, Catherine Deneuve, arguably the world's most beautiful woman, for Chanel No. 5, arguably the world's most beautiful perfume."*

Catherine Deneuve—impeccably turned out in a perfect black dress, sleek black silk stockings, elegant black pumps, and perfectly coifed blond hair held back by a black satin bow—walks into view. In her arms she cradles a large, very content looking muskrat. The muskrat is also elegantly turned out in a gleaming black leather collar studded with sparkling studs and hardware.

Deneuve (with a charming French accent):

> *"I wear ze Chanel No. 5 because it contains more extract of a muskrat's anal gland than ze next leading brand."*

Deneuve looks down lovingly at the giant rat in her arms and gives it a heartfelt, affectionate squeeze. The rodent gazes up at her with his beady little rat eyes, winks, and smiles beatifically as Deneuve strokes its coarse fur. The image fades into the product shot.

# *No, no, no, no, no!*

It's all wrong. Women don't wear Chanel No. 5 because they want to smell like a rat's ass. They wear it because they want to be sexy, loved and attractive.

Which is why you can imagine this commercial instead:

Announcer (with the same elegant English accent):

*"And now, Catherine Deneuve, arguably the world's most beautiful woman, for Chanel No. 5, arguably the world's most beautiful perfume."*

Catherine Deneuve is once again impeccably turned out. But this time she cradles an oversized bottle of Chanel No. 5 in her arms.

Deneuve (with her still-charming French accent):

*"I do not simply wear Chanel No.5 … I place it where I want to be kissed."*

With this she sticks one perfectly manicured blood-red fingernail into the bottle, throws her head back with an expression of wanton pleasure, and dabs the perfume on her swan-like neck, curvaceous clavicle, and perfect shoulders.

Yeah, baby—now THAT'S more like it!

Perfumeries know that sex (which can most certainly be classified as an emotional issue, can't it?) sells. After all, while it might be the right amount of pheromones that make the perfume work, it's the result of those pheromones that makes us want to buy the fragrance in the first place.

Why? Because *Hearts Then Minds* makes it so.

## The Center of the New World

A few years ago, Miami hosted the Summit of the Americas, a meeting that brought together the leaders of all the democratic countries in the Western Hemisphere. Because my advertising agency handles the Greater Miami Convention and Visitors' Bureau, we worked on the Summit and I was lucky enough to be invited to attend many of the speaker sessions.

As you might imagine, the speakers were the best of the best. After all, most of them were invited because of their public personas. All of them had spent years and years working on their public speaking skills. To give you an idea of the magnitude of the roster, I watched speeches by United States President Bill Clinton, President José Maria Figueres of Costa Rica, President Carlos Saul Menem of Argentina, and President Jean-Bertrand Aristide of Haiti.

Each of them was a wonderful speaker who captivated everyone in the huge convention hall. Clinton presented himself as the leader of the free world and spellbound the room with a personal charisma that made each person in the audience think Clinton was speaking directly to them.

Menem, too, was a strong personality and awed the room with a show of sophistication and worldliness. Figueres of Costa Rica pounded his fist on the lectern and controlled the audience with a fiery display of passion. But it was the humble speech by Haitian President Aristide that I'll remember forever.

After his contemporaries had set the room afire with the bigger-than-life power of their personalities, Aristide walked quietly from behind the podium. A small, humble man dressed in a simple dark suit, white shirt, and black tie that hinted at his clerical roots, Aristide clasped his hands behind his back and addressed the crowd.

"In Haiti," he said in a voice no louder than a whisper, "we are happy. And why are we so happy, you may ask yourself? Are we happy because we have food?" He shook his head slowly. "No, no. Sadly, we have very little food in Haiti. Many Haitian children go to bed hungry."

"Why are we so happy, then, you may ask yourself. Are we happy because we have abundant natural resources?" President Aristide shook his head slowly again. "No, Haiti is a barren island. We have very few natural resources."

"So why are we happy, you may ask yourself again? Are we happy because we have superior medical facilities, a robust economy, or a promising future? No, I am sorry to report that Haiti is a very poor country. We have none of those things that the rest of the western world takes for granted."

Aristide paused and looked at his shoes before continuing.

"In Haiti," he carried on, even more slowly and quietly, "we are happy because we have friends. We are happy because we know that the rest of the world now knows about our problems and will join together and help us."

And with this, almost magically, one swollen tear slid slowly down Aristide's cheek.

There may have been only one tear on Aristide's cheek, but there were many more on the faces of most everyone in attendance. And most of the people crying were savvy politicians and street-smart journalists, not a group you would think would be so quick to fall under a government leader's spell.

Aristide instinctively knew that he'd have plenty of time during the summit to explain the facts and verify his points. But before he could do that effectively, he had to reach people's hearts and make them want to care about what he was talking about.

And that is exactly what he did. Because Point #2 *Hearts Then Minds* had worked its magic on everyone in the room.

# Point #3 *Make It Simple*

We're taught that knowledge is power. The more you know, and the more your can learn about something, the better decisions you can make. Unfortunately, in the new world of access to almost unlimited information, knowledge isn't always power—sometimes knowledge is just plain confusing.

It's knowledge, properly applied, that creates power.

The Internet gives us the ability to download pages and pages of information on almost any subject imaginable. And high-speed printers make it easy for us to produce reams and reams of facts and figures. But without the talents of a knowledgeable editor—someone who can help us decide what's worth reading—all of this information is nothing more than a data dump.

As information architect Richard Saul Wurman wrote:

"Information anxiety is produced by the ever-widening gap between what we understand and what we think we should understand. It is the black hole between data and knowledge, and it happens when information doesn't tell us what we want or need to know."[4]

[4] Information Anxiety by Richard Saul Wurman, 1989

For Point #3 *Make It Simple*, to work, judicious paring is essential, as is an understanding of the most important part—the essence—of what a message can deliver and what a listener wants to receive.

But just paring down your message is not sufficient. Brevity is often reached at the expense of understanding and meaning. Reducing with skill is akin to honing a knife edge—applying the proper pressure and angle at the whetstone can result in a razor sharp edge. But if you push too hard, even the finest carbon steel will lose its edge and end up too dull to cut through anything.

While it may be intoxicating and fulfilling to pare down a message to its simplest elements, what often happens is that the spine gets pulled right out of the message along with everything else. The best way to *Make It Simple*, but still make it count, is to find the essential quality of your communication and hammer it home. And it's worth spending some time talking about how to do this.

And after all, you can't hammer a nail in sideways, can you?

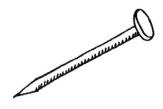

## *Just Do It*

Nike knows how to make it simple.

When Nike looked to the Wieden + Kennedy advertising agency to create a new advertising campaign, they inherently understood why people wore their athletic shoes. They understood the emotional response most Americans had to exercise (Point *#2 Hearts Then Minds*). Nike knew that most people were quite aware of the fact that they needed to exercise. After all, they read about it in magazines, heard about it on radio and television, and got the message from their doctors.

But Nike also knew that despite all the reminders, people weren't actually working out.

"I can't exercise because I have two children and I don't have time."

"I can't exercise because I work too hard."

"I can't exercise because I'm too old."

"I can't exercise because I'm too sick."

Almost everyone had an excuse. And even though all of those excuses were different, they all had the same effect—people felt guilty because they weren't working out.

So along came the smart folks at Nike and they said "Just do it." And they let us do it any way we wanted to (Point #1 *All About Them*).

They didn't tell us to "Just do it" because their shoes were cheaper.

They didn't tell us to "Just do it" because their shoes were better looking.

They didn't tell us to "Just do it" because their shoes had special cushioning or design features or custom sizes.

They simply said: C'mon along. "Just do it." And lo and behold, we did!

Reebok, on the other hand, told us "Life is short. Play hard."

Or, in other words, Reebok told us: "You're going to die soon. But before you do, get off your duff and get moving."

Nike went on to create the most successful athletic shoe company in history because they knew how to reduce their communications to present the essence of what they were offering.

Fact is, the company estimates that 70 to 80% of Nikes sold never see athletic activity. But it doesn't matter that most of us wore our Nikes while we lay on the couch channel surfing on the big screen TV.

What matters is that we're wearing Nikes. Which means we *bought* Nikes.

How can you learn from Nike's incredible success and reduce your message to its most fundamental attribute? It's as easy as taking a walk through your favorite art museum.

## The Difference Between Sculpture & Painting

 Sculpture and painting are both similar art forms—artists use their skill and vision to transform blank canvases or slabs of rock into pieces of art. Both sculpture and painting can be used realistically, abstractly, or almost any way in between. And both can create incredibly moving pieces of art.

Yes, sculpture and painting are related art forms. But they are also very different.

Take a minute and list some of the differences between the two art forms. Then read down the list and see if there are any differences that you'd add to this inventory or to your own. (C'mon, really do make the list before you read further. My example works better that way.)

### Dimension
Most painting is two-dimensional while most sculpture is three-dimensional.

### Materials
A painter uses paint and a surface such as canvas or paper. Sculptors work with stone, wood, metal, glass, wax, and other plastic materials.

### Tools
Painters tend to use brushes, chalk, and sponges, while sculptors usually work with hammers and chisels, saws and welding equipment.

## Weight

What else did you think of? Size? Footprint? Value? Life span? All of those are correct. And yet none of these differences is the most important one.

## Process

The biggest difference between sculpture and painting is the production process—they are exactly opposite activities. Most painting is additive; most sculpture is subtractive.

Think about it—a painter sets up his canvas and proceeds to put things, generally paint, onto the surface. Regardless of the technique, whether the painter is as precise as Raphael and applies the paint with single-hair brushes or as frenetic as Jackson Pollack and hurls the paint at the surface, the result is intrinsically the same. The painter continues to add paint to the face of the canvas until he's done.

The sculptor, on the other hand, takes things away from the medium until he is left with his art. This reduction process refines the original shape of the medium into whatever it is that the artist wants his final sculpture to represent.

Have you ever talked with sculptors about their work? You might have noticed that when they discuss their art, they often refer to their process as freeing the image from the marble, wood or whatever material they've worked with.

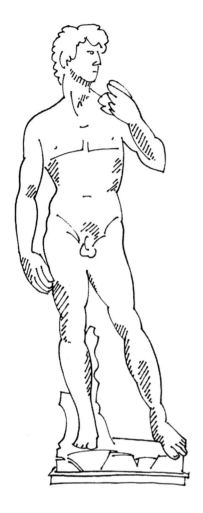

### Michelangelo, Picasso and Gary

"The driftwood knew what it wanted to be," my sculptor friend Gary said when I complimented him on a piece of art he had completed. "It was meant to be."

Or, "The bird was already in the piece of stone. It was my job to set it free."

Gary's art was contemporary, but his comment was anything but. What I discovered was that this concept is rooted in the history of sculpture.

Have you seen Michelangelo's David in Florence? Do you remember what was on either side of the hallway leading to the great masterpiece? Big blocks of partially carved marble that Michelangelo had begun to work on but soon abandoned. Apparently, as he chiseled his way into each piece of rock, he realized that David simply wasn't in there.

Or, as Michelangelo himself said:

# "I saw the angel in the marble and carved until I set him free."[5]

Then there's the famous story about Pablo Picasso: One day a student of Picasso's visited his garret to find the famous artist walking around a large slab of stone. The student watched until his curiosity got the best of him.

[5] Michelangelo Buonarroti, 1475-1564.

"What are you going to do with that big stone block?" the student asked.

"I'm going to carve a lion." the master answered.

"How will you do that?" the student asked again, clearly impressed and puzzled. "It looks really hard."

"Actually it's easy" Picasso said. "I'll take this hammer and this chisel and remove everything that doesn't look like a lion."

Well, it's the same with crafting messages. Take advertising for example—most of the ads you see and hear are like paintings—they're additive. Agencies and clients add headlines, photographs, body copy, and logos to the surface of their ad until they're convinced that they've included everything that could ever interest their potential customers. Then, perhaps they add a few more things, such as hours of operation, locations, and a few discounts—just to make sure they haven't missed anything.

Unfortunately, what they ultimately miss is their intended target's attention.

Creating specific concepts, points or messages, on the other hand, is a lot like creating sculpture. When you form your message, you decide what you want to say and then you remove every single extraneous element from the message until you're left with the single sharpest point that will get your intended target's attention.

At the same time, editing that is done without a good understanding of the issues at hand tends to dumb down most subjects to the lowest common denominator. After all, less may indeed be more, but often, less is actually less. As Frank Lloyd Wright once said: "Less is more only when the more isn't very good."

## Sometimes Simple Can Be Too Simple

In medieval England, a vagrant was arrested and sentenced to death by stoning. When the hapless convict was asked what his last request would be, he said he wanted to give something back to the community that had been generous enough to support him. He wanted to create a final farewell meal for the entire village.

The vagrant asked his neighbors to give him a large cauldron of water, a blazing fire, a rock, and three days to prepare the feast.

Needless to say, the simple townsfolk were skeptical. But seeing as how they were in the middle of a famine and they could just as easily enjoy the stoning in three days as they could today, they agreed to the vagrant's odd request.

Dressed in tattered rags that barely kept out the cold, and dragging the heavy chains that shackled his legs, the unfortunate vagrant combed the countryside for just the right rock, discarding this one for being too large, the next one for being too round, a third for being both too small and too square. Finally, after an exhaustive search, he found the rock he proclaimed to be "just right."

Returning to the town square, the vagrant set the rock into the cauldron and announced that three days hence the village would enjoy the best rock soup they'd ever eaten.

While he was waiting, he struck up a conversation with one of the observers. "Where else have you made rock soup?" the observer asked.

"Now let me see," he began. "I've made rock soup in Cornwall, Oxford, Wales, and Eaton. Although as I recall it, the rock soup I made in Eaton was one of the most delicious because it was special."

"How so?" a woman in the crowd asked.

"Well," the vagrant continued, "one of the good farmers in Eaton had an extra sack of barley that he was generous enough to share with his neighbors, and so we made a wonderfully rich barley rock soup."

"I've got some barley hidden in my barn," a farmer exclaimed. "I'm sure the King's men will claim it for themselves if they find it, but I'd be happy to put it in the soup and share it with everyone." And with that, the farmer hopped on his cart and trotted off to his farm. He retrieved the barley, brought it back to town, and poured it into the boiling cauldron.

"Barley rock soup is just wonderful," said the vagrant as he stirred the mixture. "But the best rock soup I've tried came from Cambridge, where we also added chicken and fresh carrots."

"I've got a few chickens," said a farmer.

"I've got carrots," said another. And off they went to fetch the various items that they threw into the pot.

Before long the cauldron was teeming with corn, potatoes, beef, lamb bones, and all the other foodstuffs the wily vagrant was able to cajole out of the townsfolk.

When the three days had passed, the pot was overflowing with a wonderfully fragrant stew that fed the entire village. The vagrant, now a hero, was not only set free but was offered the hand of the King's daughter in marriage along with all the riches he could carry.

## Lies Of Omission Are Still Lies

Okay, so maybe the vagrant wasn't an outrageous liar. He did promise the village a delicious cauldron of soup and the only ingredients he required from the authorities were a pot, some water, a rock, and some time.

And he delivered on his promise.

But of course the vagrant never could have produced the steaming pot of stew if the townspeople hadn't contributed all of their produce to his cause. And while the people in the story were happy with the outcome, and didn't mind, or didn't notice, that they had been tricked, the people you communicate with won't be nearly as forgiving.

How many times have you been involved in a negotiation of some sort and found to your dismay that you and the other person weren't expecting the same outcome? It's almost impossible to have a productive conversation when the receiver and the sender have different thoughts on what needs to be discussed and what needs to happen. You're promising one thing, they're listening for something else, and neither party finds satisfaction from the exchange.

Worse, there's often a third party, a competitor, further mucking up the works. You'll find this most often when you're competing for an assignment—an engineering project, perhaps, or a landscaping job, and the price or the deadline is in question. You are promising a complete project, and estimating all of the components that a comprehensive estimate requires, and your competition is offering Rock Soup. That is, your competition is presenting a proposal that looks complete but isn't, and because of their omissions, there's just no way you can offer a competitive price.

While they may have *Made It Simple* by reducing the components of their proposal, they have not included all the necessary components to successfully complete the job. And instead of "less is more" their less is actually less.

Overcoming this obstacle and winning the assignment is much easier than it seems. The key is to level the playing field by establishing a list of deliverables. That way, the recipient of your message knows what to look for in your proposal and also has an easy way of comparing it to your competition's offer.

Checklists, punch lists, inventories, schedules of deliverables, and menus are all excellent ways of helping your listener compare apples to apples. As you'll see when we get to Point #6 *All Five Senses*—it's best to engage as many of your audience's senses as possible. Remember to enumerate your roster of items. Counting off ingredients on your fingers while speaking, showing pictures of the various components, holding up examples, or illustrating the production process with the actual parts you are going to use are all good ways of strengthening your point.

*Making It Simple* is all about finding the simplest, most powerful message that can help your audience distinguish you from the competition. Then they will understand, appreciate, remember and act.

# Point #4 *Make It Quick*

"...I apologize for writing you such a long letter, but I simply did not have the time to write you a short one."

$$-George\ Bernard\ Shaw$$

## *Reduce. Reduce. Reduce.*
## *Then Reduce Some More.*

Thoreau wrote:

"Simplify, simplify."

But if he truly thought this was the best strategy, he would have written:

"Simplify."

## *What Have You Done For Me Next?*

There's no question that the world is moving at a quicker pace every day. While physicists and astronomists might point out the rotation of the earth has actually slowed slightly over the millennia, what's happening on the planet has only gotten faster and faster. Technology has made it possible to continually increase the pace of everyday life.

Think of it this way: Before fax machines and e-mail, most written correspondence was created on typewriters and delivered to recipients via the postal service. There was a built-in lag time between the beginning and end of most every engagement. Making just one change to a document meant that at least an entire page had to be retyped.

Each advance in document creation, duplication, and transmission, from electric typewriters and Quips (very early facsimile equipment) to high-speed copy machines, faxes, overnight delivery, e-mail, and instant messaging has upped the time ante considerably.

Today it's not unusual to hear software developers talking about completely rewriting their code to speed up processes by mere nano-seconds.

Just a few years ago, when Roger Bannister was the first human being to break the four-minute mile, runners were world-renowned for besting their predecessors by a tenth, or perhaps a hundredth, of a second.

Today, software that cuts process time in half, often from an already lightening fast two seconds to a 50% faster one second is not just commonplace, but expected.

Just when it seemed as if things wouldn't get any faster than a fax modem transmitting a word-processed document over an ISDN line, the Internet became ubiquitous and changed the rules of the game again.

Now instant information is available from all over the world. Transmission speeds and access times have gotten so fast that at the time this book was written, a web page download time of more than three to seven seconds was considered unacceptably slow. Who knows how fast web pages will load by the time you read this?

For years FedEx promoted themselves with the line, "When it absolutely, positively has to be there overnight." But in a world of fax machines, T1 lines and instant messaging, overnight just wasn't fast enough and the company changed their tagline to "Relax. It's FedEx."

While people's access to information has changed, the way people measure time has changed too. Time was once seen as a flowing river, moving along at its own lazy, inevitable pace. Now, thanks to date books, TV Guide grids, and palmtop PDAs (personal digital assistants), time is seen as a grid on a spreadsheet complete with slots to be organized and filled. No longer are people content to sit and wait to see what comes, instead they are trained (and driven) to fill each slot on their grid with activities, entertainment, and meaning.

Because of this, taking time to meander to a conclusion is no longer an effective way to communicate. People won't sit around and chew the fat. They want to get to the point, find out what's in it for them, and move on.

Television commercials that took sixty seconds in the 1960s and 1970s were cut to thirty seconds in the 1980s and fifteen seconds in the 1990s. And they continue to get shorter and shorter. In 1998, in fact, padlock manufacturer Masterlock even aired one-second commercials.

And television viewers, who have demanded that their shorter and shorter attention spans be titillated with shorter and more exciting programming, often use the channel-change button on their remote controls to watch bits of three or four shows at a time.

Newspapers and magazines once offered thoughtful stories that provided insight and background on a succession of pages. Now they imitate their electronic counterparts with quick sound bytes and multiple points-of-entry coverage known as "chunking." Pick up a magazine such as *Men's Journal, Wired, People, InStyle,* or *Departures* and you'll see that you can open to any page and find something short and quick to enjoy without wading through pages of text.

The bottom line is this: if you want someone's attention, say it quickly.

# Point #5 *Make It Yours*

## *Fun Fun Fun On The Autobahn*

There are five major automobile brands manufactured in Germany: Opel, Mercedes-Benz, BMW, Volkswagen, and Audi. Each company makes a comprehensive line of cars and sells them based on the quality of their design, their heritage, and their performance.

Interestingly enough, none of the companies spend much time talking about what a car actually does. Even though the basic reason for buying a car is to get from point A to point B, this simple need doesn't give consumers any reason to choose one car brand over another. And because most auto purchasers already want to drive a car, they don't need to be convinced that an automobile is a better transportation solution than a bike, a bus, or a boat.

Because of the innovations made in the automobile industry over the last 100+ years, all five German car manufacturers build fine products. Computerized fuel injection and engine management systems have made traveling 100,000 miles without a tune-up the norm for all of their cars. Advances in aerodynamics have made the teardrop/jellybean shape of most modern cars ubiquitous.

Modern cars have come so far in the last twenty years alone that an inexpensive Toyota Tercel manufactured in the mid-1990s can outperform a 1960s vintage Ferrari in almost every category. Unfortunately for auto manufacturers, offering similar products does not help them sell cars. If all cars offer essentially the same level of performance and luxury, and if all cars look and feel essentially the same, why should consumers choose one car over another? Once cars and the transportation they provide become commodities then the car companies lose their emotional bond with consumers.

To maintain this bond, the various car companies employ all sorts of consultants and marketing professionals. They hire advertising agencies, designers, and public relations consultants and charge them with the task of creating and furthering their brand. The brand positioning that professionals agree on (such as Volvo's "Safety") best represents the car company to its customers, and accurate or not, becomes the mantra used to sell the companies' products.

One of the ways that companies promote their brand is through their logo or brandmark. And Germany's five-car companies are no exception. Take, for example, each company's entry in the near-luxury division: Opel sells the Senator (it was sold as the Cadillac Catera in the USA); Mercedes-Benz, the C-class; BMW, the Three Series; Volkswagen, the Passat; and Audi, the A-4. Each of these cars is similar in specifications and features and each stands within an inch or two of the others in all important measurements.

Not only do the cars built by these five manufacturers look similar and perform almost identically, but if you were blindfolded and placed in one (and hopefully not driving), you'd be hard pressed to tell which car you were in. Opulent creature comforts such as leather interiors, multi-speaker stereos, and automatic climate control systems have raised the indulgence ante of all but the least expensive cars to such high levels that regardless of their cost, most new cars compete in the semi-luxury category.

Look on the front of each of these cars and you'll find the manufacturers' logo lovingly placed in the center of the grill. Look carefully and you'll notice that even their logos are alike. They are so alike, in fact, that I wonder how they were created. Maybe each company started with circles and did something like this:

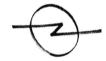

*Opel took the circle on their grill and divided it in half.*

*Mercedes divided their circle in thirds.*

*BMW divided their circle into quarters.*

*Volkswagen didn't divide their circle into fifths as you might imagine, instead they divided it into sixths. To do so, they took the Mercedes-Benz logo, rotated it 180°, removed the vertical bar and replaced it with a "W".*

*And Audi looked at all of their competitors' logos, figured there was no point in dividing their logo into sevenths, and instead just used the other guys' circles.*

The logos are almost the same!

But each logo stands for something very different:

• Opel stands for durability.

• Mercedes-Benz stands for sophistication, elegance, and engineering.

• BMW stands for performance.

• Volkswagen stands for youthfulness.

• Audi stands for design excellence.

The logos represent cars that are more alike than they are different, and as we've seen, even the logos themselves are quite similar. Yet it is the distinctive and singular positioning of each car brand that sets the automobiles apart.

Mercedes' 3-pointed stars and the cars they are attached to are indeed perceived as sophisticated and expensive—and these same attributes are bestowed on the drivers of those cars. When BMW puts its white and blue propeller on the front of an automobile, the car instantly takes on an air of high performance—"The Ultimate Driving Machine". And its driver, too, is seen as someone with taste, panache, style, and money.

Each of these positionings works because it is ownable (Point #5 *Make It Yours*), essential (Point #4 *Make It Quick*), simple (Point #3 *Make It Simple*), and because they've been used again and again (Point #7 *Repeat, Repeat, Repeat…*).

All of the other aspects necessary to make the positionings successful (Point #1 *All About Them*, Point #2 *Hearts Then Minds*, and Point #6 *All Five Senses*) have been attributed to the symbols through the car companies' constant advertising and promotions.

## *You Aren't What You Eat*

Products are no longer bought simply because of what they do. As we have seen, the five German automobile brands all provide high-quality transportation. But because of the commoditizing of both quality and transportation, the brands have to use other communication strategies and tools to set themselves apart and make their products more desirable to consumers. And the companies do this by selling their automobiles not based on what the cars can do, but based on what their vehicles offer the user.

Just like rap star Flavor Flav, who wore giant Volkswagen and Mercedes Benz logos around his neck, drivers of those cars wear their automobiles as fashion statements. They don't just buy the car—they buy into the lifestyle and the image that comes along with it.

Being a BMW driver means something more than just being a person who drives a BMW. It means you can afford the car, it means you care about the design and performance that the car offers, and it means that you are a consumer of expensive, high quality goods.

Driving an Audi means something too. Audi drivers are seen as serious, design-oriented consumers who are unconventional in their thinking (though not as unconventional as Saab drivers who respond to the advertising taglines "Find Your Own Road" and "The State of Independence") and more interested in quality and value than status (ironic, isn't it?). And Mercedes Benz drivers are concerned with quality, status, and durability and like to believe that they are value-conscious as well.

In short, the old expression *You Are What You Eat* has been rewritten. Today it is

# *You Are What You CONSUME.*

In order to take advantage of this *You Are What You Consume* phenomenon when you create a strategic positioning, the benefit you promote to the user must be yours and yours alone. Because people who accept your message will internalize it and use it to build their own self-image, it is critical that they associate all of the product's benefits with your message.

I use an Apple computer because I'm an iconoclast. I vacation in Miami because I'm hip and trendy. I vacation in Kissimmee because I want my family to be happy. I wear Brooks Brothers suits because I'm conservative. I wear $700 Manolo Blahnik stiletto heels because I'm rich and sexy. Or I wear $65 Rockport oxfords because I'm sensible and value-conscious.

If your message is accepted by the receiver, it will be embraced and proudly worn as a badge of honor. Listeners will repeat your message as if it were their own and they will use it to promote their own sense of well being and their personal identity.

# Point #6 *All Five Senses*

## *Cinnamon Buns and Chocolate Chip Cookies*

I recently read an article published by the International Council of Shopping Centers (ICSC) that claimed that while only 8% of people who were interviewed when they walked into a shopping center said they were planning to eat something in the mall, over 80% of shoppers interviewed on their way out said they had indeed eaten something.

Obviously something changed their minds.

Of course, some shoppers just got hungry, some were enticed by the displays of food, and some realized how much easier it would be to grab a treat at the mall rather than head home and start cooking. But others got caught by Point #6—*All Five Senses*. If food displays are always inviting, beautiful displays of food combined with wonderful aromas are even more tempting.

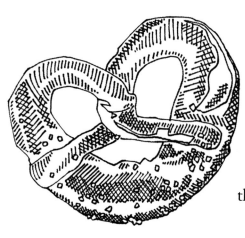

Perhaps the 92% of our shoppers who had no intention of eating in the mall would have ignored the various food stands if the restaurants had only presented their foods visually. But a large group of our shoppers weren't able to overcome the offerings because of their delicious scents. After being drawn into the bakery by the wonderful smells, our shoppers saw the great looking food and were convinced to get in line to buy a cinnamon bun or a slice of pizza.

"Dunkin' Donuts is the first national company credited with using the scents of their coffee and baked goods to attract customers and sell their products. Mrs. Fields Cookies, Starbucks and Cinnabon have all followed suit. Cinnamon is still one of the most important flavoring agents and scents in Western and Eastern societies, especially with the current craze for flavored coffees, spicy ciders, body scents, and the ever-alluring aroma of Cinnabon at U.S. malls."[6]

Clearly the wonderful smells wafting from the in-mall bakeries make their goods much more desirable. And a large percentage of the 80% of shoppers who wind up eating in shopping centers unconsciously agree.

We already know that perfume companies take advantage of Point #2 *Hearts Then Minds*, so it should come as no surprise that they also use Point #6 *All Five Senses*, in their advertising. Perfume companies know that their messages are much more compelling when consumers can look at the beautiful images in the ads AND smell the scents, so they include scent strip inserts in their magazine advertising. That way, while consumers are enjoying the fantasies suggested by the models and fanciful situations, they can also enjoy the scent of the moment.

[6]Professor Arthur C. Gibson, 1984, UCLA course on economic botany, "Plants and Civilization."

Restaurants and food companies could offer scent strips that give you an idea of what their meals smell like. Burger King ads could present the fast food chain's key differentiator—flame broiling—with scent strips doused with the tantalizing aroma of flamed broiled beef.

Tourist destinations could let you smell their locale—Barcelona could spice up their ads with the smell of olives, Provence could use lavender, Hawaii could use coconut oil, Aspen could use the fresh smells of the pine forest, Miami could use tropical fruits and Cuban coffee. In fact, the Imagineers at Disney World already target consumers' senses—one of the rooms in their Magic House at Epcot Center is scented with the just-out-of-the-oven aroma of chocolate chip cookies.

Taken a step further, car companies could let you smell the fragrant leather of their interiors and motorcycle companies could let you smell the fresh air of the open road.

But it's not just the sense of smell that can be enticing in communications. Movie producers use music to great effect to set a scene. The Muzak company gave birth to a new industry when they discovered that specific sound tracks could increase retail sales. Supermarkets use flavor when they set up sampling tables in their aisles to let shoppers taste new products. And politicians use touch when they shake hands and kiss babies.

Think about the rash of television commercials that use famous rock and roll hits from the '60s and '70s (Cadillac with Led Zeppelin, Nike with John Lennon, Levis with Nina Simone, to name just a few). Advertisers who want to reach baby boomers realize that playing these great songs can get consumers to associate their products with the good feelings the boomers felt when they originally heard the music. As soon as the first familiar notes are played, listeners' memories are transported to an earlier time—they thought about whom they were with and what they were doing when they first heard these tunes.

The next time you're making a presentation, take advantage of Point #6 *All Five Senses*. Add music to set the mood, show a clip from a video to drive a point home, offer samples or snacks. Distribute scented oils or other fragrances to add a subtle atmosphere to the room. Whatever you come up with, get your audience to use as many of their five senses as possible and you'll find it much easier to convince them of your point of view.

While we're talking about appealing to your audiences' senses, don't forget that your body language will also go a long way to make impressions and establish opinions.

## The Defense Attorney

It was the defense attorney's last chance to keep her client off death row. She smoothed her papers and her nerves and strode purposefully to the front of the courtroom.

"This closing argument," she began, "will probably be one of the most important I've ever delivered. Why? Because my client's life hangs in the balance. I'm sure you can imagine the responsibility that's resting heavily on my shoulders. But I am not worried. I'm not worried because this closing argument will also be one of the easiest I've ever given. As you've seen, there is absolutely no evidence that my client committed the murder he's been accused of. There's no weapon. There's no motive. There's not even a body. No one is even sure if the victim is indeed dead or if he's just missing."

All of the jurors listened raptly. The prosecutor sucked his teeth and looked down at his shoes.

"If I only create reasonable doubt in your minds, you must find my client not guilty." The defense attorney paused, looked around the room, and continued. "Just reasonable doubt, because the law says that in order to convict, you must believe in my client's guilt beyond the shadow of a doubt. Which means if the victim happened to walk into this courtroom right now…"

The defense attorney turned her face toward the back of the courtroom, and pointed at the suddenly opening door. With a gasp, the jurors, the judge, the prosecutor and the court reporter all looked up in time to see the elderly courtroom bailiff shuffle into the room.

"There!" the defense attorney said triumphantly. "You all thought the victim might have been coming through that door. You have all proved that there is a reasonable doubt. Now you must find my client not guilty."

She sat down. Closing arguments were over.

The judge gave her final instructions and the bailiff escorted the jurors into the jury room. It wasn't long before they were back. The bailiff guided them into the jury box. The foreman of the jury handed the slip of paper with the verdict up to the judge who read it, nodded, and handed it back.

"How do you find?" the judge asked.

"We find the accused…guilty of murder in the first degree," the foreman answered.

The defense attorney shot out of her seat. "This is an outrage," she cried. "The law says that you can only convict my client if you can do so beyond the shadow of a doubt. Obviously you have some doubt that my client committed murder. Otherwise you wouldn't have looked up to see if the victim was actually walking in the door when I suggested it."

"Makes sense," the judge agreed as she turned to the foreman. "How do you answer that?"

"Well, we all felt the same way," he answered. "We even discussed that because if we had looked to see if the victim was coming in the door then we each must have had some question as to whether he was dead or not…"

"And you all looked!" interrupted the defense attorney.

"Yes we did," the foreman continued "We all looked. So did you, your honor, and so did the court reporter. Even the prosecuting attorney looked."

"So how can you convict? You all looked."

"We all looked," the foreman agreed quietly "but the accused didn't."

## *How To Make Body Language Work For You*

When you're appealing to all of your audience's senses, remember the power of body language. We all use it and we all interpret it, yet few of us understand it or are even conscious of it.

After you finish reading this chapter, try a little experiment to prove the importance of body language. Put this book

down and go look in on your family or a few of your friends or coworkers. Start a conversation with them, or join in an existing one and try to position yourself directly in front of one of the people in the room. Once you are clearly in their line of sight, cross your arms in front of your chest while you talk to them. You'll notice that the person you're talking to will also cross their arms. After a while, uncross your arms and place them casually at your side. Before long, the person you're talking to will also uncross his arms, although you'll notice that it will take him longer to uncross his arms than it took him to cross them.

After a few more minutes, scratch the corner of your mouth or wipe your cheek. The person you're talking to will counter by touching his face too. And if you put your hands in your pockets, he'll probably do the same.

What's happening is that you and the person you're talking to are carrying on an unconscious conversation with your bodies. When you cover your chest with your arms, you're signaling that you are feeling uncomfortable or vulnerable and that you have to protect yourself. Your actions make your partner feel the same way and he'll cover his torso too. When you uncross your arms and lower them to your sides, you are indicating that you no longer feel threatened and that the other person can relax as well.

Point #6 *All Five Senses*, reminds us that there are many ways that people internalize information—through their eyes, their ears, their mouths, their noses, and with their hands and the rest of their bodies. To communicate well, it's important to interact with as many sensory organs as possible.

# Point #7 *Repeat, Repeat, Repeat...*

W e've all heard the three parts of a successful speech:

*Tell them what you're going to tell them.*
*Tell them.*
*Tell them what you've told them.*

If you've ever heard someone give a speech who followed these three rules but did it badly, you know just how boring it can be to hear the same thing over and over. But if you've ever listened to a speaker who followed the three steps and did it well, you know just how convincing and powerful this paradigm can be.

Because our minds are so busy, it's hard to focus on any one message, let alone think about the message, remember it, and act on it. There are too many other things—schedules, phone numbers, problems, hopes and dreams—competing for our attention. And it's just too easy to get distracted and not pay attention, even to something interesting.

That's why the best communicators know that it's up to them to make sure that they present their message every chance they get. Being single-minded and focused gives a message the time it needs to settle in and take effect.

## *You Can Count Them On One Hand*

As you've probably realized by now, I think my children are pretty special. And of course, they're very smart. Which is why when my kids were younger, it would surprise me almost every morning that they didn't remember their daily task list.

Both of them had a paper hanging on the closet door with a list of morning responsibilities they were responsible for. Before they left for school, my kids had to do five things:

1. Brush their teeth.
2. Make their beds.
3. Feed our pets.
4. Eat breakfast.
5. Get their books together and put them by the door.

The order in which they did these things didn't matter, as long as all five were done when it was time for them to leave for school. (You might have noticed that "Get Dressed" was not on the list. I wan't the slightest bit worried that my kids would go to school naked and they never let me down.)

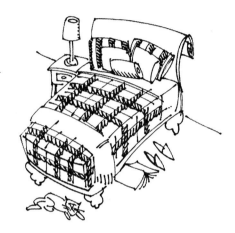

They are brilliant children and it's a simple list.

And yet every morning at my house it went like this:

*"Danny, have you brushed your teeth yet?"*

"Do I have to?"

*"Ali, it doesn't look like you made your bed."*

"I didn't know I was supposed to."

*"How about breakfast? Did you guys eat?"*

In unison "We're not hungry!"

*"And where are your books?"*

"We forgot," they say, again in unison.

Remember, my kids are brilliant. And they were only supposed to remember five things. Which is why I find it so odd that we believe that we can tell people (including those who aren't so brilliant) something once and then expect them to remember it.

*The way to get people to hear you and remember what you said is to make sure that they hear it often enough that it can penetrate their consciousness.*

## Intel Inside

Intel did it. And they did it over and over and over again.

They tacked a few seconds on to the end of almost every major computer company's television ads with a reminder to buy a computer with "Intel Inside." We've all seen the message hundreds of times. Right before the computer ad ended, we heard a catchy tune with four simple notes (Point #6 *All Five Senses*) and saw the words "Intel Inside" placed within an oval swoosh (Points #3, #4 and #5, *Make It Simple*, *Make It Quick*, and *Make It Yours*).

Although we had some idea that Intel made microprocessors, we didn't really know what an Intel was or what it did, and we certainly didn't know why we needed one. But we did accept the message that we had to have a computer with an Intel inside.

Of course the "Intel Inside" campaign worked so well because we saw it so many times. Instead of using their advertising budget to buy their own thirty-second ads, Intel created cooperative advertising with the computer manufacturers and used their money to generate thousands of commercial messages that consumers saw time after time.

# All Together Now

So what do you do with all of this information? Well, for starters, cut out the Brain Darts card on the back page of this book and stick it in your purse or wallet. And the next time you have to convince someone of something, pull out your crib sheet and review the 21 words that make up the seven simple guides.

Run over your argument in your head and make sure that it fits our seven points.

## Point #1
### All About Them

*People will listen to you when what you say benefits them. Entertain them, educate them, or enlighten them. Best of all, do all three.*

*Create a message that is All About Them. Specifically address why it's to their best advantage to see things your way.*

## Creating YOUR Brain Dart

To demonstrate that your message is *All About Them*, begin your dialogue with the benefits that you're offering to the listener.

In a conversation, this can be as easy as starting your talk by telling the listener how they will benefit from seeing things your way.

In a presentation, you might list the things your audience will learn from you and tell them how those things will improve their lives.

In advertising, it might be nothing more than showing the enjoyable results produced by your product instead of telling them why your product is better than the competition's.

## Point #2
### Hearts Then Minds

*People accept an argument or buy a product based on their emotional response— and then they justify their decision with the facts. Get someone's personal interest in your subject aroused before you try to convince them you're right.*

## Creating YOUR Brain Dart

Make sure your message reaches out to *Hearts Then Minds.* Make sure your message goes for an emotional sell before it tries to be logical or intellectual.

Make sure you arouse someone's personal interest in your subject BEFORE you try convincing them of why you're right.

## Point #3
### Make It Simple

*Instead of adding on feature after feature and muddling your message, reduce your communiqué to its simplest essence.*

*When crafting your message, Make It Simple. Reduce your argument until you're expressing the essence of what you want to communicate.*

## Creating YOUR Brain Dart

For this to work, judicious paring is essential, as is an understanding of the most important part—the essence—of what a message can deliver and what a listener wants to receive. Often, the difference between confusing your listener and making your point is the difference between filling your communications with extraneous information and getting right to the point.

Think about tourist destinations—you can describe the best known ones in just a few words: New York is urban and sophisticated; Washington DC is the seat of American government; Las Vegas is sinful; Miami is hot and sexy.

Figure out the few words you can use to get *your* point across.

## Point #4

*Be respectful of your audience's time. No presenter has ever been told, "I'd have given you the business if you'd only spoken for another hour or so." Make your point and Make It Quick.*

*As the short story author Raymond Carver wrote, "Get in. Get out. Don't linger."*

*The world is speeding up at an incredible pace. If you want someone to listen to your message, present it quickly and succinctly.*

## *Creating YOUR Brain Dart*

Brevity is often reached at the expense of understanding and meaning. But thoroughness can also hurt understanding if it stops your audience from paying attention. The best way to *Make It Quick*, but still make it count, is to find the essential quality of your communication and hammer it home.

Think back to how well the folks at Volvo understands this. Their positioning, Safety, is only one word. And their tagline, For Life, is only two.

What could be quicker than a word or two? Can you describe your unique point in only a couple of words?

Burger King says "Have it your way."

BMW is "The Ultimate Driving Machine."

WAL-MART's Brain Dart is "Always low prices. Always."

What's yours?

---

**Advertising Age magazine's**
**"Top Ten Slogans of the 20th Century"**
(Notice that none is longer than five words)

*"Diamonds are forever."*
(De Beers)

*"Just do it."*
(Nike)

*"The pause that refreshes."*
(Coca-Cola)

*"Tastes great, less filling."*
(Miller Beer)

*"We try harder."*
(Avis)

*"Good to the last drop."*
(Maxwell House)

*"Breakfast of champions."*
(Wheaties)

*"Does she…or doesn't she?"*
(Clairol)

*"When it rains it pours."*
(Morton Salt)

*"Where's the beef?"*
(Wendy's)

## Point #5
### Make It Yours

*The easiest way to create your communications is to watch your competition and copy their successes, but at best all you'll do is announce your admiration for your rival and at worst, viewers will think you ARE the competition.*

### *Creating YOUR Brain Dart*

To *Make It Yours*, be sure that everything you communicate belongs to you and you alone. If you can put your competitor's name onto your message and it fits them as well as it fits you, then your message still needs work.

Picture your communication as your receiver's identification bracelet; Once your message is accepted by your listeners they will embrace it and wear it as a badge of honor. That is, your listeners will repeat your message as if it is their own, and they will use it to help support their own sense of identity. To take advantage of this, craft a message that your audience can identify with and will feel proud to display as a banner.

## Point #6
### All Five Senses

*It's not enough to simply show something or say something. The more senses you can excite, the better your argument will be noticed, internalized, and remembered. Figure out a way to have your audience feel, taste, touch, smell, see and hear what you're saying—that's how you'll make a real impact.*

### *Creating YOUR Brain Dart*

The next time you're making a presentation, engage your audience's senses. Play music, show a video clip, offer samples or snacks or perhaps spray the room with scented oils or other fragrances to set the mood.

When you enumerate the details of your argument, try counting off the ingredients on your fingers while speaking, show pictures, hold up examples, or illustrate the production process with actual parts. All of these simple techniques are good ways of making your point stronger because they engage your audience's *All Five Senses*.

## Point #7
Repeat. Repeat.
Repeat...

*Say it and then say it again. Nobody has enough time in his or her busy day to sit and concentrate on what you're saying, so nobody's going to wait around for your message. You need to repeat it as often as possible.*

*Ironically, this is not a license to be repetitive. Instead, you'll need to muster all of your creativity to make your repeated message sound fresh and new.*

## *Creating YOUR Brain Dart*

Be sure to *Repeat. Repeat. Repeat.* If something's worth saying, it's worth repeating. Again and again and again.

Get your brand or message in front of your target as often, and in as many different ways as you can. Teach your management and staff to become brand evangelists, preaching the virtues of your company or product wherever they go. Better yet, create an army of cheerleaders who understand what your Brain Dart is and how they can spread the word.

The practice of creating Brain Darts doesn't only work in advertising but succeeds wonderfully in all interactions where it is important to get attention, get a point across, and convince the listener toward, your point of view.

# It's Not Just What You Say— It's How You Say It

Your conversations, speeches, and presentations, essays, and explanations can all benefit from *The Seven Points of Brain Darts*. When you use these seven points to create clear, direct communications, you'll achieve superior results again and again.

# Building Consensus Around
# Your Brain Dart

Before you can start selling your postitioning to the outside world, make sure the people around you buy into the idea. To get these people to understand your unique positioning, lead them through this scenario.

But try it yourself right now.

Imagine walking into an office building to make the business presentation of a lifetime. You step onto the elevator and select your floor and you're standing quietly as the doors glide shut. All of a sudden, a briefcase is thrust through the closing doors and you instinctively push the "OPEN" button to let in the businessperson who's holding the attaché. After thanking you, the new passenger notices the stack of papers in your hand and asks what you're doing in the building.

How would you explain your unique positioning in the short time you have before the elevator reaches your floor? Your new friend has asked you about something that's taken lots of your time, money, and concentration to develop, but he's only on the elevator for three more floors.

That means you have about 27 seconds—"Ding… Ding…Ding!"—to explain what you've been working on.

Your answer—which must obviously be short, sweet, and to the point (a Brain Dart, in other words) is your Elevator Speech.

Preparing your Elevator Speech in advance and having the people you work with do the same thing prepares you with a unique positioning that most everyone will agree with.

Just look around and figure out how to apply *The Seven Points of Brain Darts* when you communicate.

## A Picture Is Worth A Thousand Words

Try this little experiment: The next time you gather your family together for a photo, go through your normal routine—hold up the camera, tell everyone to say "cheese" and snap the shot. Then, tell them you want to take a second picture. This time, hold up the camera, tell everyone to say "chocolate," and snap the shot.

When you compare the photos, you'll be amazed at the difference between the shots.

Why? Well it's simple.

Remember the quote attributed to Mae West? When someone reprimanded her randy ways and said that sex was dirty and sweaty, she quipped back: "It is if you do it right!"

It's the same with saying cheese—cheese is stinky and smelly—if it's done right.

So if we want people to smile, and we want their eyes to sparkle for our photos, it makes sense to have them think about something passionate and sweet instead of something stinky and smelly.

Sure, forming the "Ch" and "ee" sounds of "cheese" can pull your cheeks up into a smile. But saying "chocolate!!" meets all seven requirements of Brain Darts: It's intimate, passionate, easy, quick, unique, sensual and easily repeated.

And it makes people smile.

Quite simply, it will work for you.

So will Brain Darts.

*Notes*

*Notes*

# Notes

Cut out the Brain Darts® card below and stick it in your purse or wallet.

The next time you have to convince someone of something, pull out your crib sheet and review the 21 words that make up the seven simple guides.

Run through your argument in your head and make sure it fits our seven points.

Contact: 305-476-3500 or bruce@turkel.info

**BUILDING BRAND VALUE**

**The 7 points of Brain Darts®**

*All About Them*
*Hearts Then Minds*
*Make It Simple*
*Make It Quick*
*Make It Yours*
*All Five Senses*
*Repeat, Repeat, Repeat...*

Printed in the United States
117874LV00006B/3-14/A